Big Valley, Pennsylvania.
A young Amish boy loads a wagon with corn to be cut for silage, accompanied
by his faithful dogs, while his brother works in the background.
Leslie A. Kelly © 1992

A Lancaster-style buggy passes a double *Doddy* house at Bird-In-Hand, Pennsylvania

AMERICA'S

AMISH COUNTRY

DOYLE YODER · LESLIE A. KELLY

Published by America's Amish Country Publications, P.O. Box 424, Berlin, OH 44610-0424. · First Edition April 1992, reprint May 1993 · Printed in Korea for Terrell Publishing
Library of Congress Catalog Card Number 91-93139 · **ISBN 0-9630590-0-9**

FOREWORD

Rexford, Montana

During a visit to Sugarcreek, Ohio, several years ago, Kelly met with George Smith of **The Budget**(™) for information on the Amish Lifestyle to use with a magazine article. In nearby Berlin, he met Yoder whose photography style in Amish Country Calendar fit in with his long considered interest in publishing a photo book about the Amish. The contemplated book would present the Amish lifestyle as part of a look at the scenic beauty of the areas in which the Amish lived and not be a photo documentary styled like those now on the market.

To complement their existing photography, Yoder and Kelly teamed up to travel to most of the Amish communities from Tennessee to Ontario, Canada, from Maryland to Oklahoma and each visited many other communities independently. The result of these years of effort is a fresh approach to presenting the Amish lifestyle in *America's Amish Country*.

During our travels, we met many Amish who were tolerant of our cameras as we attempted to record the scenic beauty of their community. Some provided information, much of which appears in the captions. Because they would not want to be credited individually, we thank them anonymously for their invaluable assistance.

America's Amish Country is the result of the blending of the best of photography styles by two internationally known photographers, both recognized in their own fields of endeavor.

Doyle Yoder grew up around the Amish of Holmes County, Ohio, and has concentrated on the scenic beauty of Central Ohio, the Amish of Ohio, Pennsylvania, Indiana and New York and trains. Les Kelly has travelled extensively across the United States photographing Americana and the Amish communities in the mid-west.

Individually, we thank our families as follows: Doyle Yoder: My wife, Valori, for tolerating my travel whether she stayed home or was able to go along with me, and my sons, Austin, Jonathan and Joshua, for putting up with Daddy being away a lot. Leslie A. Kelly: My Mother, Eblene Kelly, for her steadfast encouragement, and my children, Erin and Patrick, for their interest in *Dad's pictures*.

GEORGE R. SMITH, Hometown Editor

The Budget(TM) was a typical small town newspaper when the Smith family became the owners. George developed the idea of a publication for the Amish, and through a lifetime of work and dedication has made **The Budget**(TM) a national institution with a loyal and dedicated readership. To the readers of **The Budget**(TM), to the "Scribes" whose letters appear in **The Budget**(TM) and to those who work with him to put the paper out every week, George Smith is more than editor or publisher, George is a friend. His continued dedication inspires all of *his employees* to want *his newspaper* to be the hometown newspaper for all of the Amish communities everywhere.

George was born January 3, 1907, on a farm just north of Sugarcreek, Ohio. His father, S. A. Smith, purchased **The Budget**(TM) in 1920 and George worked there evenings, Saturdays and vacations throughout his high school years. Since then, he has been Editor, Manager and Owner of **The Budget**(TM). Although now "retired," he continues to serve as Editor of the National Edition that is comprised of Letters from the hundreds of Amish (and Mennonite) scribes who write the news from their community.

We are pleased to dedicate *America's Amish Country* to George R. Smith who has faithfully contributed to uniting the Amish communities of America's Amish country for more than seventy-two years.

THE AMISH LIFESTYLE

The horse-drawn buggy is the best known symbol of the Amish to the curious *Englisher*, *Yankee*, or *High People* (names given by the Amish for anyone who is not Amish) who stare at them from passing cars and tour buses. Known as the plain people because they wear plain colored clothing, they live in scattered farmland locations across America. The Amish—who speak *Pennsylvania Dutch* among themselves—live within highly personalized relationships, avoiding more than casual contact with strangers who might attempt to educate them to the ways of the outside world. While the Amish avoid most of the conveniences of the 20th Century, something that most outsiders have difficulty understanding, they are happy in their way of life.

AMISH ORIGINS

The Amish originated from the Anabaptist movement of the early 1500s in Switzerland. Jacob Amman, who believed in conserving traditions and separation from the world more than the other Anabaptist, led a split from the Swiss "Mennonite" Brethren in 1693.

Since the early 1700s when they first arrived in Pennsylvania as part of William Penn's "Holy Experiment," the Amish have been living a simple lifestyle in accordance with their religious beliefs.

There are approximately 120,000 Amish in North America. The largest group is in Holmes County, Ohio, with significant populations in Pennsylvania, northern-Indiana and Iowa. Others are located in the eastern and mid-western states and Ontario, Canada.

The Amish of Lancaster County, Pennsylvania, are perhaps the best known because of the many tourists who visit the area and the movie, *Witness*, which was filmed there.

AMISH AGRICULTURE

The Amish are primarily farmers. Some, however, are carpenters and cabinet makers, blacksmiths, buggy and harness makers, all geared toward supporting the Amish lifestyle. Because farmland is expensive, and becoming increasingly scarce, some younger members have taken jobs in nearby factories and restaurants. Others work in general stores that provide the

Amish community with goods necessary to their lifestyle that they cannot produce themselves.

In reality, the Amish lifestyle is very much like that of the *Englisher* ancestors of a century or so ago.

Their neat Amish farms, without electric and telephone lines, look very much like those of the *Englishers* around them. The houses are comfortable structures with numerous rooms to support typically large families.

Many of their conveniences were used in America's 19th Century or earlier houses. Wood or coal fueled stoves provide heat. Cooking stoves are powered by propane, kerosene or wood. Kerosene or clear gas lamps provide light.

A distinctive feature of America's Amish country is the windmill, used to pump water for house or farm use. While some also use gasoline engines to operate pumps with pressure tanks to provide running water for bathrooms and kitchen sinks, the old-fashioned hand pump is still used in many houses.

Some use kerosene-fired water heaters. Others run a system of pipes through the kitchen stove (fired with wood, kerosene or propane) to obtain hot water for kitchen or bathroom use.

Those lucky enough to have natural gas on their property will use it to heat their house, provide hot water, fuel their refrigerator and provide light at night.

Colorful flowers brighten the ever present "kitchen gardens." Quilts decorate bedrooms while calendars with scenic pictures, meeting the requirement of utility, cover many of the walls of their houses.

The Amish people do not pose for pictures because they believe that photographs violate the biblical teaching against making graven images (Exodus 20:4). Also, they are concerned that pictures will promote self-pride. They may put their hands or hats over their faces, look away or take evasive action to avoid having their picture taken.

Page 4: A young couple with infant daughter are on their way to church near Kidron, Ohio.

Page 5: *Left:* While flowers decorate the yard of this house near Barrville, Pennsylvania, the strict Nebraska Amish do not permit window screens or painting of their out buildings. *Above:* Two Amish men exchange greetings in Holmes County, Ohio. *Right:* A large Amish family shares a single open carriage while going to church at Seymour, Missouri.

WHAT IS AMISH?

Not every horse and buggy seen in America's Amish country may be driven by an Amish person. A number of groups share a common Anabaptist heritage with the Amish. Small, distinct sects of Brethren and Old Order Mennonites also use horse and buggies.

The Amish themselves can be generally categorized into several groups broadly defined as New Order, Old Order and a few groups more conservative than the Old Order.

Within these groups, there are numerous differences. The Old Order has the most members and are probably the most familiar to *Englishers*.

The Old Order use few modern conveniences, avoiding such things as motor driven equipment. They do use steel wheeled tractors for stationary power sources to power thrashing equipment or to pull equipment on the highway. They do not use tractors to work in the field except in hot climates where horses cannot withstand the high heat.

Some Old Order have indoor plumbing and running water.

While the New Order retain many of the Old Order traditional practices, they can be considered the most progressive of the Amish groups. Some groups may allow telephones, use air-filled tires on tractors and even allow electricity in the houses.

The more conservative groups, such as the Swartzentrubers and related groups, the Nebraska Amish of Central Pennsylvania, avoid indoor plumbing, do not use motorized equipment of any kind and wear conservative clothing.

The Nebraska Amish do not use suspenders or bonnets and are not permitted to have screens on their doors and windows.

FAMILY MOST IMPORTANT

The Amish people cherish their biological and church family. Families visit each other frequently. Distant friends and relatives remain in contact by mail and by letters to **The Budget**(TM).

Because the readers have lots of relatives with whom they wish to stay in contact, they write to **The Budget**(TM) about their family and

Above: Although they are using a horse and buggy, this Mennonite couple near St. Jacobs, Ontario, is readily distinguished by the man's lack of a beard, a certain sign that he is not Amish.

community activities. Of the 20,000 subscribers to **The Budget**(TM), 18,000 copies are mailed to Amish families.

When the older family members "retire" from farming, they move into a "Grandpa House" or *Doddy* house adjacent to the main farmhouse. They continue to work, performing useful chores around the farm, while retaining a strong sense of independence.

Amish people will not accept public welfare aid or retirement income. They do pay income and real estate taxes and are exempt from social security taxes if they farm or are self-employed.

Amish parents treat their children with deep respect and love. The children help with chores around the house and farm as soon as they are able to do so.

Until they start school at the age

of six, most Amish children speak little English. Most attend parochial schools. However, in those counties predominantly inhabited by Mennonites, many Amish children may attend public schools. Whether attending public or private schools, they only attend through the eighth grade.

The New Order church districts have taken steps to counter the Old World custom of bedroom courtship and allowing the young to "sow their wild oats" before marriage and their entry into the church.

Three older sisters lead their younger brother into the house near Milverton, Ontario.

In an effort to provide alternative social activities, similar to programs designed to keep *Englisher* youth off the streets, church ministers meet with the youth to sing hymns and talk.

The Amish are quick to help each other. *Frolics* (a work party) are held to raise a neighbor's barn or house. The men and older boys from five or six families, called a *thrashing ring* or *circle*, will help each other harvest crops.

While the men typically do the heavy farm work, the women prepare meals, make quilts and can food. In times of illness, death or disaster, the entire Amish community rallies to help.

Church rules permit only one-strap suspenders in the Big Valley, Pennsylvania.

GROUP LIFESTYLES VARY

Deeply devoted to their religious beliefs, they hold church every other Sunday at a different house in their church district (usually consisting of 25-30 families). The approximately three hour service is followed by lunch and several hours of socializing.

In this way, too, they are able to monitor the lifestyle of each family to assure compliance with the rules of the church. Those who do not are confronted. If they refuse to comply, they are shunned until they

This Old Order Amish man allows his beard to grow full-length.

either do so or are ex-communicated from the church. Amish youth usually join the church in their early twenties. They can do so earlier but must do so before they marry. They are not forced to join; however most usually do because of their strong faith in the Amish lifestyle.

"Rules of order," or the *Ordnung*, are set by the local church district Bishop. The rules which govern the Amish community cover almost every aspect of their lives. They include types of buggy wheels, length of hair for men (the women do not

Amish children help with chores around the house and farm.

cut their hair), width of hat brims, etc. This explains the variances found between Amish communities.

Some groups allow a more tolerant lifestyle than others. The clothing rules in Indiana are not as strict as those of Holmes County, Ohio.

Amish men wear beards based on a biblical passage which states that they should not mar the hair on their face (Leviticus 19:27).

Young men are encouraged to grow beards as early as possible but must do so, unless they are physically incapable, upon marriage. Old Order wear their beards longer while the New Order keep them neatly trimmed.

Because the European soldiers who persecuted them had mustaches and used large buttons on their uniforms, the pacifist Amish avoid any resemblance to the military. Amish men neither grow mustaches nor use buttons on their coats.

7

LaGrange, Indiana

AMISH BUGGY STYLES

The most obvious symbol of the Amish is their horse-drawn buggy. Buggies come in many styles and colors, reflecting the preferences of the various communities. As illustrated on this page, the traditional black buggy is not as traditional as *Englishers* may think. Various types of buggies can be equated to *Englishers'* cars and trucks. The market wagon, which has a rear panel that lifts, is closest to the station wagon. The spring wagon, or cab wagon, is the equivalent of the pickup truck.

In Lancaster County, buggies with gray tops belong to the Amish and all black buggies signify Old Order Mennonites. Other differences can be found in buggies based on the degree of conservatism of the individual church district leaders. Such differences can include windows, window wipers, battery powered head-, tail- and directional lights, rubber or steel-rim wheels, etc.

One concession to modern civilization has been forced upon the Amish buggy. After numerous accidents at night involving fast moving cars and slow moving black buggies, the Amish have added reflective tape to the back of their buggies. Less conservative groups have added battery-powered lights and installed slow-moving vehicle triangles.

Even so, some groups have refused to "adorn" their vehicle with these "loud" or "fancy" implements. In Harmony, Minnesota, the issue divided the Amish community and resulted in a State Supreme Court ruling in favor of those who had resisted their use.

9

LIFESTYLE SEEMINGLY PARADOXICAL

A number of paradoxes seemingly exist as the Amish strive to maintain their simple lifestyle in the 20th Century.

While horses pull things with wheels, some groups use gasoline engines to power agricultural implements and other equipment. Rubber wheels are replaced with those of steel and the drive shaft, designed for connection to a tractor, is fitted to a small engine by way of a pulley and belt.

Although Amish people cannot own or drive vehicles, they do travel by train or bus and ride in cars and trucks driven by others to visit friends and relatives or take vacation trips to scenic areas.

Neither electrical appliances nor telephones are found in Amish houses. They will use (public or friends') telephones to make doctor appointments, hire drivers (of vans) to take them for a doctor's appointment at a distance or to visit friends and relatives beyond a buggies' range.

They are also snow birds. There is a retreat for the elderly members in the Pinecraft area of Sarasota, Florida, where they go usually during the winter. The plain people see no problem with this since most of those who visit

Pinecraft are the older, retired people who maintain the same lifestyle as back home. Besides, it allows them the opportunity to visit with others—one of the basic pleasures enjoyed by the Amish.

AMISH POPULATION GAINING IN NUMBERS

What about the future of the Amish? It seems secure. Despite the few who leave the faith each year, their population has been gaining in total number. This is due chiefly to

Left: An Amish man uses a public telephone placed conveniently in an Amish neighborhood. *Center*: A couple is taking the train to visit relatives in another state. *Below*: This little boy, who will wear a dress until potty trained, is one of an ever increasing Amish population. *Right*: An Amish woman boils hot water and uses a wringer washing machine that is powered by a gasoline engine, with the aid of a pulley and belt.

increased longevity common to the general American population and families that average seven children.

While most immigrants are assimilated into America's culture, the Amish remain a religious community forming a subculture almost three hundred years after their arrival.

Although the Amish are seemingly a paradox in 20th Century America, they live a lifestyle that allows them to comfortably and peacefully follow their religious beliefs.

ABOUT PHOTOGRAPHING THE AMISH

Care has been taken to provide these photographs for *America's Amish Country*, many of which contain pictures of the Amish people, through nonobtrusive photographic means. We believe that it is important to show the Amish as they are, a group of people peacefully living their chosen lifestyle much like any other people, just different, in some of the most scenic country in America.

America's Amish Country focuses on scenic beauty while providing a glimpse into the Amish lifestyle. For detailed information about the Amish, we recommend *Amish Society* by John Hostetler © 1980 ISBN 0-8018-2334X, The John Hopkins University Press.

Stanwood, Michigan

OHIO

The largest community of Amish in the world is located in Holmes County and the surrounding counties of Wayne, Tuscarawas and Coshocton. There are approximately 115 Amish church districts in the area.

Pages 12-13. Neatly kept farms with large white barns, such as this one at Winesburg, are a common sight in the hills of Holmes County. **Page 14.** *Above:* Spring is in the air. Fruit trees are in blossom near Middlefield as a Geauga County-style buggy passes. *Below:* A young boy uses discs to work the soil for spring planting at Mt. Hope. **Page 15.** *Above:* Illustrating the differences that can be found among the Amish

communities, this buggy with a cooler on its roof has a white slow-moving-vehicle (S.M.V.) sign rather than the usual red color. It belongs to one of the seven church districts in Ashland County. *Lower left:* A young boy has the chore of pulling up mustard from a wheat field at Maysville. *Below:* Using a team of Belgian draft-horses, a farmer prepares his fields for spring planting in the hills of southern Holmes County near New Bedford.

16

Amish farmers raise numerous field crops, including oats, wheat, barley, corn and hay, to feed their families and animals and to sell for cash income.
Page 16. Above: Harvesting barley near Wilmot. Below: Loading hay near Bunker Hill. **Page 17.** At Berlin (above) and Charm (below), farmers raise oats, wheat and barley.

Page 18. *Above:* This school near Charm, no longer needed for its original purpose, serves as a tool shed for the practical Amish. *Center:* The Old Order Amish use push mowers like these near Middlefield. New Order Amish will use gasoline powered mowers.

Lower: Three Amish boys and their dog enjoy an afternoon of fishing near Maysville. **Page 19.** The Barn Raising. In the tradition of caring, the Amish get together to help their neighbors, *Englisher* or Amish, when tragedy or catastrophe strikes. In August 1988, two weeks after lightning caused this farm's barn to burn near Farmerstown, 700 workers came together to erect a new barn in less than one day. *Above, left:* Early morning finds the crew, directed by an older master builder, putting up the framing. *Above, right:* Amish women take time out from meal preparation to check the progress of the men. *Left, center:* The roof takes shape. *Right, center:* Workers line up to wash for the noon meal. *Below:* Children enjoy a good view of the barn raising from a nearby hill.

19

Summertime is harvest time in Holmes County. The beauty of this area makes it easy to understand why so many Amish make their home here. **Page 20.** *Above:* At Walnut Creek, a wagon load of oat shocks heads for the thrasher in a nearby barn. *Below:* Milk production is a major source of income for the Amish farmers in Holmes County. A hack returns from dropping off milk at a local cheese factory. **Page 21.** *Above, right:* Neatly kept farms, such as this farm near Charm, are a trademark of the Amish people. *Center, right:* Sunrise at Berlin finds a young boy going to work in the fields. *Below:* Sunday is a day of rest and church near Fryburg. Afterwards, these churchgoers will visit with friends and family.

Pages 22-23. Flowers are a trademark of Amish farms throughout America's Amish country. Usually silos are filled in the months of August and September with corn fodder to feed the farm animals during the winter months. The wheels on the tractor used for stationary power are all steel, as air-filled tires are not permitted.

Page 24. *Above, left:* Near Mt. Eaton, five or six neighbors of the thrashing circle help to fill silo at this farm. *Below, left:* Corn husking is a time consuming operation which requires that all members of the family help. **Pages 24-25.** Fall harvest means that fall foliage will follow soon. Fall foliage and big, white barns of the Amish combine to make a beautiful scene near Trail.

Pages 26-27. Fall is the time to drive the back roads to enjoy the foliage. **Page 27.** *Above, right:* Amish children attend school beginning in early September. Because school houses are built in the middle of the neighborhood, many of the children walk to school like these young scholars (students) at Mt. Eaton. *Center, right:* Three young girls walk home amid foliage splendor near Beck's Mill. *Below, right:* A little boy, too young for school, accompanies his father on an errand at Kidron. Because Amish parents have their children accompany them while working, a strong parent-child bond is formed.

FALL FOLIAGE IN HOLMES COUNTY.

Page 28. *Above:* Near Winesburg, a team of white horses pulls a grain drill used to plant seeds in the ground. *Below:* A fast moving buggy passes a slower draft-horse team pulling a wagon at Fredericktown. **Page 29.** *Above, left:* Near Beck's Mill. *Above, right:* Baltic. *Center, right:* New Bedford. *Below:* New Bedford

Page 30. *Above:* Snow covers this bridge leading to an Amish farm near New Bedford as a young girl waits her turn to sled. *Below, left:* School is out! Children who live near the school walk while others living at a distance use horse and buggy. *Below, right:* Like school children everywhere, these young scholars take advantage of their lunch break for a few fast rides on the hill. **Page 31.** *Above, left:* Buggies travel through heavy snow at Charm. *Above, right:* Farm work continues in the snow at Mt. Eaton. *Left, center:* A wagon is used to make a trip to the feed mill near Mt. Hope. *Below:* A winter's storm covers buggies parked at the Mt. Hope livestock auction. *Right, center:* A warm late-winter sun starts the sap flowing in the sugar maple trees at Beck's Mills. Some Amish farmers tap their maple trees and boil the sap in "sugar shacks". Maple syrup is a special treat at an Amish table. Excess syrup may be sold or given away.

Lancaster County is the most widely known of
the Amish areas in the U.S. Pennsylvania
has the second largest population of Amish
scattered over much of the state.

Pages 32-33. An Amish carpenter passes an
empty school house early on a Saturday while
on the way to help build a new house in
Lancaster County. Because there is a shortage
of farmland in Lancaster County, many
Amish must find alternative jobs to farmwork.

Page 34. For the Amish, attending church at
the house of one of the district's members is a
bi-weekly opportunity to worship and socialize
with their families and neighbors. Girls and
boys walk up the drive to the house, passing
several "social" mules that have come close to
watch the parade of buggies and people.
Women and girls enter the house while the
men and boys wait in the barn until their cue
from the Bishop to enter. Inside the house,
benches are arranged so that women, girls and
infants are seated on one side and boys and
men on the other. **Page 35.** *Left, below:* The
little girl of the host house makes a last sweep
of the driveway. *Above and right, center:*
Buggies arrive for service. *Right, below:*
About 9 a.m., the older boys enter the house
where they will be seated separately from the
women and girls. Finally, the youngest boys,
accompanied by their fathers, enter. Soon
after, the melodious sound of Amish hymns,
sung *a cappella,* fill the air.

35

Page 36. In an apparent contradiction to Amish conduct, the Amish raise tobacco as a cash crop although few smoke. This farm is at Strasburg. Page 37. An Amish family returns to their home after a social function at a neighbor's house. Page 38. *Above:* Farmers use horse-drawn motorized mowers at Intercourse. *Left, below:* Reminiscent of the past, a gray-topped Lancaster buggy enters Jackson's Mill covered bridge. *Right, below:* A woman picks berries for the family table near Georgetown. Page 39. *Above:* Although he is barely old enough for school, this little boy near Quarryville already knows how to handle the mules. *Left, center:* Two white mules pull a sprayer as the sun sets at Intercourse. *Left, below:* A farmer checks his corn field before spraying. *Right, below:* Corn is a major crop for the Amish in Lancaster .

Page 40. In the Big Valley (Kishacoquillas Valley), there are black, yellow-topped and white-topped buggies. Men use only one suspender strap to hold up their pants. The Big Valley is considered to be one of the most scenic settings in all of America's Amish Country. *Below:* A wagon with corn for silage heads home to this large farm. Page 41. *Above:* Two yellow-top buggies carry a family visiting in the Big Valley near Belleville. *Center:* A team of horses prepares a field for planting at Belleville. *Lower:* A Nebraska Amish, considered to be the most conservative of all Amish, works in a field near Barrville. The men wear brown pants tied in the back, without suspenders, and a white shirt.

41

Page 42. Snow comes to the Big Valley every winter. *Above:* A farm sparkles in the bright sunshine at Belleville. *Center:* Amish children enjoy sledding on a Sunday afternoon near Belleville. *Below:* Spring in the Big Valley is a time of flowers, sunshine and beauty. The Nebraska Amish are also called "white-toppers" because of their buggy tops.

Page 43. *Above:* A young Nebraska Amish boy and his father go to the auction in Belleville. There they may buy a new draft-horse, farm implement or other equipment needed on their farm. *Right:* An Amish man and woman consider a purchase at the weekly auction. *Left, below:* School boys chat and clown around during recess at Belleville.

Page 44. *Above:* The five church districts at Summit Mills in Somerset are the only Amish to use a church meeting house (outside of Pinecraft in Florida). *Center:* Brown- (or rust colored) topped buggies are used by the twelve church districts around New Wilmington. *Lower:* Surrounded by colorful fall foliage at Smicksburg, a farmer hauls corn stalks for fodder to feed his cattle during the winter months. **Page 45.** A Somerset County buggy passes under spectacular foliage on a mountain road near Summit Mills on a beautiful fall day.

INDIANA

Indiana is the home of the third largest population of Amish in the United States. With 94 church districts in northern Indiana, the Amish have large settlements in LaGrange, Topeka, Shipshewana, Middlebury and Nappanee. The farmland of northern Indiana is virtually flat with only a few small hills to accent the landscape.

Pages 46-47. Near Shipshewana, late summer flowers paint a pretty picture at this large farmhouse and barn. Note the huge bell on the windmill tower which is used to summon men in from the field.

Page 48. *Above:* This typical farmhouse near Shipshewana has a long, white fence, a flower garden and three clotheslines to hold the wash of the large family living there. *Below:* Two young heifers, an important source of cash income for their owner, graze in a field of summer clover near Topeka.

Page 49. *Above:* A buggy makes its way past a field of shocked oats in front of a large farm near Montgomery in southern Indiana. The eleven (11) church districts there have only recently adopted the use of top (covered) buggies. *Center, right:* Outhouses, flower gardens and windmills are a familiar sight around Shipshewana. *Below:* A team of white horses pulls a hay cutter in a field near Berne. This field may yield up to three cuttings of hay each season. Farmers use it to feed their cows and horses during the winter months.

Page 50. *Above:* Top buggies are not permitted among the twenty-two (22) church districts in Adams County. This family, passing a colorful stand of day lilies, uses an open buggy. *Center, left:* A square backed buggy takes a young couple visiting near Shipshewana. *Center, right:* A girl hitches a ride at Nappanee from a slow-moving church-bench wagon. These wagons are used to store benches between Sunday services. This farmer is moving it to the next family's house to host church services. *Below:* A buggy travels a scenic road near Nappanee.

Page 51. *Above:* Two men paint the neighborhood school near Topeka. *Center, left:* The Amish around Shipshewana use steel wheels on their wagons. In the background is the "Shipshe" Auction where livestock sales are held weekly and a major flea market operates. *Center, right:* A buggy passes a Mennonite neighbor's farm near Shipshewana. *Below, center:* A man's straw hat and a little girl's dress are on display at the Honeyville General Store where many Amish shop for their store bought goods. *Below, right:* This quilt being sewn in a home near Topeka will make a handsome gift when completed. Amish women form sewing circles to make quilts for friends and family, fund raisers and for sale to tourists.

Page 52. *Above:* Field work is in full swing at Nappanee. Grandfather and grandson work together to cultivate their corn field. *Center:* Most of the teams at work in this hay field are Belgians, the draft horse favored most by the Amish. *Below:* Two girls pick strawberries for a family treat. **Page 53.** *Above:* Huge corn fields are the rule around Topeka. *Center:* Gasoline engine powered hay balers are permitted at LaGrange while in nearby Howe (below) the more conservative Amish put up their hay loose.

Page 54. *Above:* Walking to church, an Amish couple does the "Amish shuffle" while crossing a puddle in this rain soaked road at Geneva. *Center:* This farmer is stocking up with coal to use in heating his home near Topeka. *Below:* A young family heads for church services at a neighbor's house near Berne.

Page 55. *Above:* Fog obscures three draft horses as the sun rises near Topeka. *Center:* The City of LaGrange has installed a block long hitching rack at the LaGrange County Courthouse, one of the prettiest in all of America's Amish country. *Below:* Colorful fall foliage frames two buggies near Shipshewana.

The gently rolling hills around Kalona, in southern Iowa **(Page 56)** contrast with the flat land of Buchanan County **(Page 57)** in central Iowa. Iowa is home to the fourth largest population of Amish. They have settled in the major areas of Kalona, Bloomfield, Milton and Buchanan County. **Pages 58-59.** *Above:* At Bloomfield, an Amish man uses a road cart to run a quick errand. **Page 58.** *Below:* This buggy is typical of the style found among the eight church districts at Kalona. **Page 59.** *Center:* Tired from the day's activities, a little boy naps on the way home at Fairbank. *Below:* An "Amish weedeater" takes a break near Milton.

Harvesting field crops is a neighborhood project in July. Threshing rings members work together to complete the harvest. **Pages 60-61.** At Kalona, young boys take water to the men shocking oats. This large field was shocked in less than six (6) hours. The shocks will be allowed to dry for several weeks before being taken to the threshing machine. **Pages 62-63.** *Above:* Working in the company of his faithful dogs, a farmer operates a binder in this field at Milton. **Page 62.** *Center:* Farm work is learned at an early age as the young ones pitch in to help Dad. *Below:* The day's work complete, horses and farmer head for home near Fairbank. **Page 63.** *Below:* The setting sun behind a thunderstorm paints the sky over a harvested field of oats as a herd of dairy cows returns to pasture after their evening milking.

Page 64. *Above:* Hay is loaded and put up loose in Buchanon County. *Below:* Soybeans are harvested with a grain binder by Amish farmers near Fairbank.
Page 65. At Hazleton, an approaching thunderstorm gives meaning to the old saying, "Make hay while the sun shines!"

Pages 66-67. Near Jamesport, a man rides horseback for a quick trip to a neighbor's house. Some consider riding horseback to be showing off which explains why it is rare to see an Amish man on horseback.

Pages 68-69. *Above:* A power wagon, a diesel engine with a large-wheel, is used to power a combine near Clark. Some Amish groups permit the use of these stationary power sources to run farm equipment.

Page 68. *Below:* Four Belgian horses pull an oat binder at Jamesport as neighbors help with the harvest.
Page 69. *Below:* A farmer uses a hack at Seymour to visit a neighbor's house.

Page 70. Chores are an important part of growing up for Amish children. *Above, left:* Near Clark, a young boy uses a horse to herd cows into the barn for the evening milking. *Below, left:* A boy drives a team to the field for a day's work at Canton. *Above, right:* Their day's chores completed, three boys take time to fish in a pond at Jamesport. *Center, right:* Every Amish settlement has at least one sawmill. This small sawmill overlooks the Ozark Mountains at Linneus. *Below, right:* A schoolhouse near Windsor is ready for young scholars (students) to return. **Page 71.** *Above:* Silhouetted against a setting sun, a boy hitches a ride home after working in a field near Jamesport. *Below:* At sunset, a young couple in a hack pass a pond at Seymour.

Page 72. *Above*: At Seymour, two boys deliver the morning milk to the collection station. A tank truck will take the milk for processing and distribution at a local dairy. *Center*: Colorful clothes hang on the line to dry at Jamesport. The women and girls are responsible for taking care of the clothes in this large family. *Below*: Five teams of horses pull hay mowers in this field near Jamesport. **Page 73:** A lone hack starts down a long hill east of Jamesport.

Page 74-75. Storm clouds bring welcome rain for crops in the fields near Cashton, largest Amish settlement with seven church districts. **Page 76.** *Above:* Young boys follow behind a binder stacking shocks of freshly cut oats at Cashton. *Below:* Early morning clouds hang over a team of Belgian horses ready for a day's work in a field. **Page 77.** *Above:* An Amish couple work together to cultivate their garden at Cashton. *Center, left:* Amish children are expected to follow in their parent's footsteps. A close-knit bond develops between father and son. *Center, right:* Their work interrupted by rain, a father walks while his children ride home on work horses near Cashton. *Below:* An Amish mother hangs up clothes to dry while her daughters prepare their horse and buggy for an errand.

78

Page 78. *Above:* Flower gardens, like this one near Pardeeville, add bright colors to yards throughout America's Amish country. *Below:* A wagon load of hay is destined for the next barn at Medford.

Page 79. *Above:* Near Cashton, a father and his children walk home. *Below:* A dairy herd is an essential part of every Amish farm. These cows, at Amherst, are being driven out to pasture after their morning milking.

79

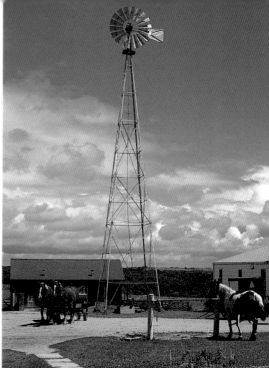

Page 80. *Above, left:* At Amherst, a threshing machine sits quietly at sunset, awaiting another busy day shortly after sunrise tomorrow. *Above, right:* A young boy's pony stands in the front yard of this typical Amish homestead at Cashton.
Below: The last rays of sunlight brightly color these huge, twin thunderstorm clouds east of Cashton. **Page 81.** At Wilton, a blue and white summer sky and a black buggy create an idyllic setting.

MICHIGAN

Page 82. *Above:* A spectacular sunrise greets early morning risers in the dairy community of Mio. *Below:* At Stanwood, flowers line the edge of a kitchen garden. The electric utility pole, leftover from its *Englisher* owner, is used by its Amish owner to hold gourd bird houses. Amish feel no need to remove electric wires to their houses so long as they are disconnected at the roof's edge. Besides, practically speaking, if the Amish sells, an *Englisher* might be the next owner. Page 83. *Above:* A lone buggy passes a huge dairy farm and school house at Mio on its way to Sunday morning church services. *Below:* Horses patiently await their owners who are attending church services.

83

Page 84. *Above:* Near Gladwin, an Amish family uses a flower lined kitchen garden to provide fresh vegetables for their table and produce to sell to tourists. *Below:* A farmer and his young son haul fresh vegetables raised on their nearby farm to sell at Stanwood.

Page 85. *Above:* A roadside stand catering to tourists in an important cash source for this family near Stanwood. *Below:* Amish life is not all work and no play as these buggies parked at a lake near Centreville indicate.

Page 86. *Above:* At Camden, with brightly colored trees behind them, a family harvests their corn field. Fall field work prepares the soil for the winter as these scenes *(center and below)* from Mio illustrate.

Page 87. Bright fall foliage and colorful pumpkins stacked up for sale make a beautiful scene as a woman and her children run an errand.

NEW YORK

Page 88-89. Travelling through a snow-created wonderland of white, a black buggy passes a row of sugar maples lined with tap buckets at Conewango Valley in this early spring scene.

Page 90. *Above:* A woman and man bundle against the winter's bitter cold. *Below:* A buggy and wagon pass under an ice-covered canopy of tree limbs.

Page 91. *Above:* Snow-covered farm implements patiently await the spring thaw. A young boy's sled, propped against the side of the barn, is ready for yet another ride down a hill. *Center:* Young scholars are called to school by their teacher. *Below:* A buggy passes by the schoolhouse.

Page 92. *Above:* Conewango Valley is one of the most scenic areas in America's Amish country. *Center, left:* A milk hack returns from the delivery station at Woodhull. *Center, right:* At Jasper, a boy uses a team to fill silo. *Lower left:* In Conewango Valley, a young boy brings in the cows for their evening milking. *Lower right:* Surrounded by mountains at Conewango Valley, a horse teams pulls an oat binder. **Page 93.** *Above:* Young boys and their dog pass a manure cart pulled by a handsome pair of horses at Conewango. *Center:* In Clymer, a hay rake and buggy are parked ready for their next use. *Lower:* Children take a hack to school near Heuvelton on a cold, fall morning.

ILLINOIS

The Amish in Illinois live in the area around the village of Arthur. **Pages 94-95.** Strong Belgian horses are used to work in the fields. **Page 96.** *Above:* A trip down the road to visit a neighbor is a major part of the Amish tradition of the eighteen church districts at Arthur. *Below:* Flat farm land is characteristic of central Illinois. **Page 97.** *Above:* This spinning rake is preparing cut hay for baling. *Below:* The last rays of the fading sun color these oat shocks with a golden glow.

Page 98. *Above:* Flowers add color to a kitchen garden at Arthur. *Below:* A long day in the hay field lies ahead for this team of Belgian horses.

Page 99. *Above:* Sunlight streams through the fog over a colorful flowerbed. *Center, left:* After shopping in Arthur, this Amish mother readies her horse for the trip home. *Center, right:* Young girls go out for an early morning ride. *Below:* Oats are an important farm crop as this picturesque setting shows.

Page 100. *Above:* The very conservative Swartzentruber Amish inhabit the rolling farm land of southeastern Minnesota near Harmony and Canton. None of the buggies here have the slow-moving-vehicle triangle because the Amish resisted their use and won in the Minnesota Supreme Court. *Below:* Amish youth help with farm chores from an early age. A boy herds the family's cows toward the barn for the evening milking at Harmony.
Page 101. *Above:* Children often accompany their parents on a shopping trip to Harmony. *Below:* A surrey, a two seated buggy, adds to the scenic beauty of the hills surrounding Harmony.

100

Page 102. *Above:* Near Harmony, an Amish man and his son use a stationary power source mounted on a small wagon to power a blower to fill their silo with hay. *Below:* A farmer uses a gasoline engine-powered sprayer at Saratoga.

Page 103. *Above:* Old equipment sits in a field, like museum pieces, at Wadena, home of a small settlement of Amish. *Below:* A child's wagon, at Canton, standing beside a large wagon with logs, is used by a small boy to imitate his father's work.

Page 104. At Mechanicsville, the Amish raise tobacco as a cash crop. *Above:* Amish men work alongside hired helpers to harvest tobacco for sale. *Below:* This farmer has hung an early crop of tobacco to dry in a curing barn.
Page 105. A young girl rides with her father in a hack just after sunrise near Mechanicsville.
Page 106. *Above:* A woman hangs her morning wash next to a field of sunflowers at Mechanicsville. *Below:* Near Grantsville, a little boy and girl, holding hands, help herd the family cows in for their evening milking. Even though they live in Mary-land, this group of Amish belongs to a Somerset County, Pennsylvania, church district.
Page 107. A long lane leads across the gently rolling land to a farmhouse at Mechanicsville. The gray top on the buggy indicates that this group came from Lancaster County, Pennsylvania.

DELAWARE

108

Page 108. *Above:* The Amish hack serves the same purpose as the *Englisher's* pickup truck. *Below:* The Amish who settled in Delaware in 1915 developed their own distinctive buggy style with a rounded bottom. There are eight church districts near Dover. **Page 109.** *Above:* Amish teenagers work many long days in the fields of their father's farms. *Below:* A farmer does his spring plowing with a team of five Belgian horses.

Page 110. *Above:* Wild mustard contrasts with a black, round-bottomed buggy near Dover. *Below:* Colorful—but plain—clothing is used throughout America's Amish country.

Page 111. *Above:* These cows, as in many Amish communities, are an important source of income for their owners. *Center, left:* While some New Order groups permit the use of gasoline powered lawn mowers, only push mowers are allowed at Dover. *Center, right:* Little fellows wait for Mom at the local store. *Below, left:* A local carpenter finishes up a church bench for use at Sunday service. *Below, right:* Girls help Mom with a trip to the mail box.

Page 112. *Above:* A young boy learns by watching his father operate a horse-drawn corn planter at Ethridge. *Below:* Preparing the fields for spring planting is a common scene in April. **Page 113.** *Above:* An Amish man walks home for lunch after a morning spent painting. *Below:* The local Amish blacksmith prepares to shoe an *Englisher's* horse at Huntingdon.

Page 114. *Above:* The sun creates lacy shadows under a tree at Ethridge. *Below:* The Amish farmers at Ethridge are not permitted to use balers so they must put up loose hay. **Page 115.** *Above:* A young boy does the spring plowing in this field. The church benches stacked on the front porch of the house are an indication that church or a special ceremony has recently taken place or will soon take place at this house. *Below:* The self-reliant Amish plant large "kitchen" gardens, usually tended by the women of the house. Here, an older son uses a team of horses to prepare the ground for spring planting.

KENTUCKY

Page 116. *Above:* At Marion, Kentucky, the settling group of Amish purchased 5,000 acres of land. They built their own roads without bridges, requiring horses and buggies to ford the creeks. *Below:* At the new community of Gradyville, getting the crops in at the right time is more important than finishing the house. **Page 117.** *Above:* The very conservative Swartzentrubers use a simple buggy style around Park City. *Below:* A young couple drive their open buggy in the rain past Yoder Road at Marion on their way to church.

Page 118. *Above:* A team of Belgians pulls a wagon at Gradyville. The rounded bottom of the following buggy signifies that this settlement of Amish came from Dover, Delaware. *Below:* A buggy passes by a colorful field of spring wildflowers at Marion. **Page 119.** *Above:* A young Amish family travels to visit friends at Glasgow. *Below:* A buggy splashes through a creek just before sunset at Marion.

KANSAS

Page 120. *Above:* There are three Amish church districts around Yoder. *Below:* A spectacular sunset colors the sky above the Kansas plains.
Page 121. *Above:* The flat land of Kansas makes easy pulling for a horse hitched to a buggy. *Below, left:* A full moon rises over a parked buggy at Mont Ida, home to two church districts near Garnett. *Below, right:* Locals and visitors alike are welcomed to Yoder. Horse-drawn buggies are used for transportation but tractors are used to work the fields in the hot weather of Kansas.

OKLAHOMA

Page 122. *Above:* Bright colored clothing is hung to dry under fluffy early morning clouds at Chouteau. *Below:* Horse-drawn buggies still ply the roads around Chouteau but field work is performed with tractors. **Page 123.** *Clockwise, above, left:* A family walks home from church past a large field of yellow flowers at Clarita. *Above, right:* An ingenious use of old farm equipment makes a great place for this beautiful array of flowers near Chouteau. *Center, right:* Some Amish have had telephones installed outside their homes with large bells to attract their attention when a call comes in. *Below:* An Amish farmer plows his field with the aid of a tractor. The extreme heat of Oklahoma is very hard on horses. *Left:* Young folks gather behind the local feed mill to socialize.

Page 124. Rexford was settled by the Amish when fifteen (15) families joined together to buy 3,000 acres from an estate sale. They have established a thriving "tourist" trade from vacationing Amish from the eastern states as well as a pre-fabricated log house business. Living in a big valley at the Canadian border, not far from Lake Koocanusa, they also grow hay and harvest timber in the nearby mountains using horses.

Page 125. *Above:* Mt. Robinson dominates the valley to the west.

ONTARIO

The Amish of Ontario, Canada, have settled in the eastern provincial towns and counties around Aylmer, Lucknow, Chatsworth, Milverton and Millbank.
Page 126. A farmer operates a hay rake in the foreground while a wagon follows with a hay loader (*above*) near Lucknow. **Page 127.** Sitting almost 20 feet above the ground, a farmer passes dairy cattle on the way to deliver straw at Mossley. **Page 128.** At Aylmer, flowers brighten a farm yard.

Page 129. *Above:* Two girls load oat shocks on a wagon while their younger brother drives a team of horses at Millbank. *Below:* Their father backs an empty wagon from the barn to unload oats that his children have brought in from the nearby field.

Page 130. *Above:* "Farm fresh" never had truer meaning as a father-son team prepares the soil for a late summer crop just meters away from their produce stand at Aylmer. *Left:* Nearby, another farmer takes to the road to sell his produce. Page 131. *Above:* With pitch forks reaching toward the setting sun, a farmer hauls the last load of the day to the threshing machine at Millbank. *Lower left:* Near Desbro, a buggy starts down a long, scenic hill. *Lower right:* At St. Mary's, a mother and her young daughter return home from visiting a neighbor. The "kitchen garden," in the foreground, provides the family with fresh vegetables.

TEXAS

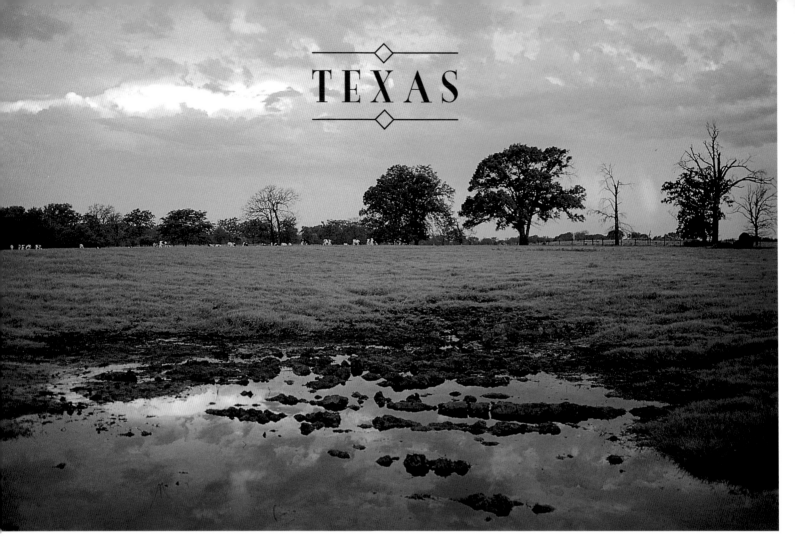

A small group of Amish families have settled near Sulphur Springs, Texas, in the communities of Como and Pickton. They work on dairy farms owned by *Englishers* and do not farm for themselves. **Page 132.** *Above:* Dairy cows graze while an early morning thunderstorm colors the sky with a rainbow at Como. *Below:* An Amish man uses a road cart to visit the next farm at Pickton.

PINECRAFT AMISH CHURCH

Amish "snow birds," usually elderly Amish, visit the Pinecraft area of Sarasota, Florida, each winter. **Page 133.** *Above:* A bicycle (or tricycle), instead of a buggy, is the accepted mode of transportation for this elderly couple vacationing in Florida. *Below:* The Pioneer Trails bus, so-called the "Amish Express," carries winter travelers from the major communities in the north to Sarasota on a weekly basis during the winter months. *Inset:* Because the houses in the Pinecraft area are typically small the Amish have selected one big house, which càn accommodate a large crowd to serve as their permanent church building.

133

CREDITS

Leslie A. Kelly: Two page fold out, 1, 2, 3, 4, 5 left and right, 6, 7 above, below and right, 11, 32-33, 35 above and below left, 39 below left, 41 above, 46-47, 48 above, 50 center left, 51, 54 center, 55 above, 58-59 above, 60-61, 62 above, 63, 70 center right, 72 below, 82, 83, 84, 85 above, 86 center and below, 87, 92 center left, 93 below, 100 below, 101 above, 102 below, 103, 104 above, 107, 114 above, 115 above, 118 below, 119 above, 123 top left, center right and below, 124-125, 128, 129 above, 132, 134 lower left and right, Back cover, Jacket photo of Doyle Yoder and Les Kelly, Back end sheet.
All photos © 1992 Leslie A. Kelly

Doyle Yoder: Front cover, three page fold out, 5 above, 7 left, 8, 9, 10, 12-33, 34, 35 right center and below right, 36, 37, 38, 39 above, center left and below right, 40, 41, 42, 43, 44, 45, 48 below, 49, 50 above, center right and below, 52, 53, 54 above and below, 55 center and below, 56, 57, 58 below, 59 center and below, 62 center and below, 64, 65, 66-67, 68, 69, 70 above left, above right, below right and below left, 71, 72 above and center, 73, 74-81, 85 below, 86 above, 88-91, 92 above, center right and below (both), 93 above and center, 94-99, 100 above, 101 below, 102 above, 104 below, 105, 106, 108-111, 112, 113, 114 below, 115 below, 116, 117, 118 above, 119 below, 120, 121, 122, 123 above right and center left, 126, 127, 129 below, 130, 131, 133, 134 above left and right, 135, 136.
All photos © 1992 Doyle Yoder

For comments about *America's Amish Country* or for information about other America's Amish country publications, write **America's Amish Country Publications**, P.O. Box 424, Berlin, OH 44610-0424

New Bedford, Ohio

Big Valley, Pennsylvania.
A young Amish boy loads a wagon with corn to be cut for silage, accompanied
by his faithful dogs, while his brother works in the background.
Leslie A. Kelly © 1992